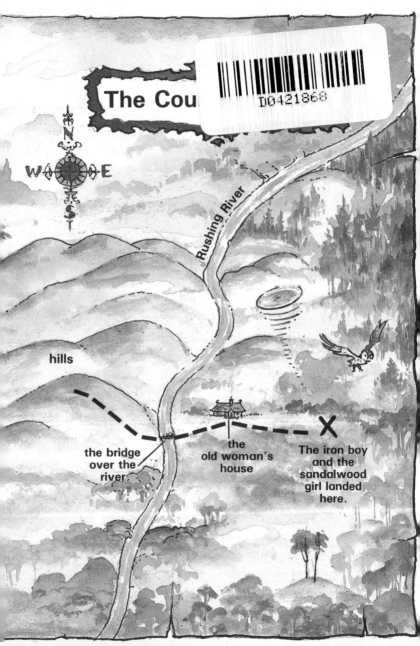

USING THIS BOOK

One of the best ways of helping children read is to read stories to them and with them.

If you have been reading earlier books in this series, you will be used to reading the story from the left-hand pages only, with words and sentences under the illustrations for the children to read.

In this book, the story is printed on both the left- and right-hand pages.

The first time you read the book, read the whole story, both left- and right-hand pages, aloud to the child and look at the illustrations together.

The next time the book is read, you read the text on the left-hand page and the child, in turn, reads the text on the right-hand page, and so on through the book.

LADYBIRD BOOKS, INC.
Lewiston, Maine 04240 U.S.A.
© Text and layout SHEILA McCULLAGH MCMLXXXVI
© In publication LADYBIRD BOOKS LTD MCMLXXXVI
Loughborough, Leicestershire, England

All rights reserved. No part of this publication may be reproduced, stored in a retrieval system, or transmitted in any form or by any means, electronic, mechanical, photocopying, recording or otherwise, without the prior consent of the copyright owners.

Printed in England

On the Way to the Blue Mountains

written by SHEILA McCULLAGH
illustrated by JON DAVIS

This book belongs to:

W|||RAM

Ladybird Books

There was once an old house
in Puddle Lane.
The house had a clock, in a little tower.
A bell hung under the clock.

A boy, made of iron, stood by the bell.
He had a silver hammer,
and he struck the time on the bell.
But one night, at twelve o'clock,
the iron boy struck the bell thirteen times.
And, suddenly,
he found that he could walk!

The iron boy knew that a magician
lived in the house.
He climbed down the roof and
went to see the Magician.
The Magician sent him
to the magical Country of Zorn,
in a flying saucer.

This story tells what happened
when he got there.

4

The iron boy lay in the flying saucer,
looking down over the edge.
The moon was shining down,
and he could see that the saucer
was flying over a great forest.
It seemed to take a long time,
before the forest came to an end,
and the flying saucer flew down,
and landed on the grass
in the Country of Zorn.

The iron boy climbed
out of the flying saucer.
He looked all around him.
The moon was shining down.

He was standing at the edge
of the forest. In front of him,
he could see rolling hills.

The iron boy looked back
at the trees.
A big owl
flew over the treetops.

The iron boy hid in the shadow
of a bush and watched.

The owl flew down to the grass,
near the iron boy, and
a girl climbed off his back.

"Goodbye, owl, and thank you,"
the girl said softly.

"Goodbye," cried the owl.
"The moon is going down.
You must go west,
toward the moo-oo-oo-n!"
And he flew up into the sky.

The girl looked around her.
The iron boy stepped out
into the moonlight.

11

"Who are you?" cried the girl.
She sounded frightened.

"Don't be afraid," said the iron boy.
"I'm a boy, made of iron.
I used to strike a bell,
on a clock in Puddle Lane.
But one night,
I struck the bell thirteen times,
and I found that I could walk.

"I went to see the Magician
who lived in the house,
and he sent me here,
to the Country of Zorn."

"I know you!" cried the girl.
"I lived in the house in Puddle Lane.
I heard the clock strike thirteen.
I went to see the Magician, too.
The Magician sent me here,
on the owl's back."

13

"I came in the Magician's flying saucer,"
said the iron boy.
"I'm looking for the Blue Mountains.
I want to be like other boys.
The Magician said that
if I wash in the Silver River,
which is in the Blue Mountains,
I won't be made of iron any more.
I will become really alive,
like the boys in Puddle Lane."

"The Magician told me to find
the Silver River, too," said the girl.
"I am made of sandalwood.
I want to be like other girls.
I must wash in the Silver River, too."

"Then let's go and look for
the Silver River together,"
said the iron boy.
"The Magician said
that it would be a dangerous journey.
It will be safer for two,
than it would be for one.
Will you go with me?"

"Yes, I will go with you,"
said the sandalwood girl.
"The owl told me to go west,
where the moon is going down."

"Let's do what the owl said,"
said the iron boy.

They set off together, over the grass.

The iron boy went first.
He stamped the grass down
with his iron feet,
so that the sandalwood girl
could walk along easily.

They had not gone far, when
they saw a light ahead of them.

The light was shining out
of the window of a little house.
"Let's go to the house,"
said the iron boy. "We can ask
the way to the Blue Mountains."

They went to the door of the house
and knocked.

"Who's there?" cried a voice.
"Who is knocking on my door,
at this time of night?"

"A boy, made of iron, and
a girl, made of sandalwood,"
said the iron boy.
"We are going to
the Blue Mountains.
Can you tell us the way?"

A very old woman opened the door.
She had white hair and brown eyes.
She had a red shawl.

She looked at them kindly.

"Dear me!" she said. "Are you all
alone? It's a long, long way
to the Blue Mountains.
And it's a dangerous journey."

"But we must go," said the iron boy.

"Come in and sit down,
and I'll tell you the way,"
said the old woman.

The iron boy and the sandalwood girl
went inside the little house,
and sat down beside the fire.
(The sandalwood girl was careful
not to sit too close to the flames.)

"Now tell me about your journey,"
said the old woman.

And she looked so kind, that
the sandalwood girl told her
the whole story.

"Stay here until the sun comes up,"
said the old woman.
"Then you will see a river,
at the bottom of the hill.
You must go down the hill
to the river."

"It isn't the Silver River, is it?"
asked the sandalwood girl.

"No, no," said the old woman.
"It's the Rushing River.
You will see a bridge.
You must cross the bridge,
and follow the path
that you find on the other side.

"The path will take you to the top
of a hill. From the top of the hill,
you can see the Blue Mountains.

"But be careful.
The bridge is very old,
and the Rushing River is very deep."

The iron boy and the sandalwood girl
stayed with the old woman until
the sun came up.

Then they went outside,
and looked down the hill.
They could see the Rushing River
at the bottom of the hill.
It was very wide, and very full of water.
There was an old wooden bridge
over the river.
They could see a path
on the other side,
leading up to the top
of a big hill.

The iron boy and the sandalwood girl
said, ''Goodbye, and thank you.''
Then they went down to the river.
They came to the bridge.
It was a very old bridge,
and it was full of holes.

They stepped onto the bridge.
The bridge shook under them,
but there was no other way
to cross the river.
"Watch where you put your feet,"
said the iron boy. "Don't fall in.
I'm made of iron, and if I fell in
I would sink to the bottom
like a stone."

"I'm made of wood,"
said the sandalwood girl.
"I can swim. I'll go first,
and see if the bridge is safe."

So the sandalwood girl went
over the bridge, and
the iron boy went after her.

They had just reached the middle
of the bridge, when the iron boy
caught his foot in a hole, and
fell down with a crash!

The bridge broke.
The iron boy and the sandalwood girl
fell down into the river!

The sandalwood girl grabbed
the iron boy as they fell.
(She remembered what he had said
about sinking.)
She held on tight to the iron boy
as they splashed down into the water.

The river was running very fast,
but the sandalwood girl
didn't let go.
She sank down under the water,
but she didn't let go
of the iron boy.

She pushed her head up, out of the water.
She pulled the iron boy's head out, too.
She began to swim.

"Kick with your legs," she said
to the iron boy.
"It will help keep you up."

So the iron boy kicked out
with his legs, and the sandalwood girl
held on to him. She just managed
to keep their heads above water.

The river was running very fast.
The water splashed over
the sandalwood girl, but she didn't
let go of the iron boy.

Her arms began to ache.
She was getting very tired.
Just when she thought that
she couldn't hang on any longer,
the iron boy said,
"I can feel the ground!
One of my feet is on the stones."

A tree was growing by the river.
The iron boy grabbed
a root of the tree.
The sandalwood girl climbed
out of the water,
onto the root,
and the iron boy climbed up beside her.

"We are safe!"
said the sandalwood girl.
"We are safe on the other side."

They climbed along the tree root,
and onto the grass on the riverbank.
Then they sat in the sunshine to dry.
They could see the bridge.
The bridge was so broken, that
they couldn't have gone back,
even if they had wanted to.
So as soon as they were dry,
they climbed the hill,
just as the old woman had told them to.

When they came to the top
of the hill, they stopped.
They stood still, and looked.
Far away, very far away,
they saw the Blue Mountains.

Notes for the parent/teacher

In the books in Stage 4, the child is asked to read part of the story and not just the sentences under illustrations. This is a big step forward.

If you read the whole story to the child first, it will make the reading much easier for her.* But some children still need the chance to read quietly to themselves the pages that they will later read aloud with you.

Reading a story aloud on sight, without having had a chance to look at the text first, is one of the most advanced and difficult kinds of reading. When the child is reading aloud, if she reads the words in such a way that the story makes sense but the words are not exactly the same as those in the book, don't correct her on the first reading. If she does it the next time you read the book together, you might ask the child to look a little more carefully. For example, if the child reads "the sun had gone down," instead of "the sun had set," let it pass on the first reading. This kind of mistake shows that the child understands the meaning of the printed text, even though she gives that meaning in her own

---

* In order to avoid the continual "he or she," "him or her," the child is referred to in this book as "she." However, the stories are equally appropriate for boys and girls.

words and not the words in the book. Even skilled readers do this sometimes. On later readings, ask the child to look carefully at what was there in the book.

If a child gets stuck at a word, you can simply say what the word is. There are also three useful ways of helping a child discover what the word might be:

(a) looking at the illustration for clues;

(b) reading the sentence again from the beginning after the child has looked at the picture;

(c) skipping the word the child doesn't know and reading on to the end of the sentence.

If she still can't "guess" the word, or if she shows any sign of becoming worried, tell her what the word is.

Remember always that both you and your child should **enjoy** your reading sessions. Figuring out a word she doesn't know should be almost a game from the child's point of view. Approach words in this way yourself, helping the child look for "clues."

Keep the book, even when the child can read her part of it easily and has gone on to other, more difficult books. Children will later reach a stage where they can read the whole story for themselves.

*The first five stories in **Stage 4** are about the iron boy who lived on the clock tower of the Magician's house and the sandalwood girl who lived in the Magician's attic. One night something strange happens and they begin their adventures in the Country of Zorn.*

Stage 4

1 When the Clock Struck Thirteen

tells how the iron boy came to the Country of Zorn.

2 The Sandalwood Girl

is the story of what happened to the girl doll, carved out of wood, who was in the attic of the old house when the clock struck thirteen.

4 Fire in the Grass

continues their adventures as they go on their dangerous journey.

5 The Silver River

tells how the children are carried to the Blue Mountains by the silver ponies. When the boy and girl have bathed in the river, they become like ordinary children and finally meet someone who tells them their names.

More suggestions for helping children read the books in this series will be found in the *Parent/Teacher Guide*.